About the Author

Ioana Onofrei is a writer and poet born in Mangalia, Romania. Coming to the UK at the young age of eleven it was challenging for various reasons, hence why she chose to lose herself in poetry books and romance novels. Using personal experiences, listening to piano keys while sipping some hot coffee represents the things that inspire her the most.

Be it Oscar Wilde, Christina Rosetti or Emily Dickinson, the romantic period was fascinating to her, with writing and publishing her own poetry book and making people get lost in her writing becoming one of her biggest dreams.

To Be Adored by Me

Ioana A. Onofrei

To Be Adored by Me

Olympia Publishers
London

www.olympiapublishers.com
OLYMPIA PAPERBACK EDITION

Copyright © Ioana A. Onofrei 2022

The right of Ioana A. Onofrei to be identified as author of this work has been asserted in accordance with sections 77 and 78 of the Copyright, Designs and Patents Act 1988.

All Rights Reserved

No reproduction, copy or transmission of this publication may be made without written permission.
No paragraph of this publication may be reproduced, copied or transmitted save with the written permission of the publisher, or in accordance with the provisions of the Copyright Act 1956 (as amended).

Any person who commits any unauthorised act in relation to this publication may be liable to criminal prosecution and civil claims for damage.

A CIP catalogue record for this title is available from the British Library.

ISBN: 978-1-80074-263-5

First Published in 2022

Olympia Publishers
Tallis House
2 Tallis Street
London
EC4Y 0AB

Printed in Great Britain

Dedication

Mama, this is for you. For your wasted tears, sleepless nights, for the times you had no idea how to help me. I am smiling now, Mama, the good times are here. I love you.

Acknowledgements

The first thanks have to go to the woman who always believed in me and showed me unconditional love and support. Thank you, Mama, for everything.

To my amazing friends who have showed me support and believed in my talent. Jack, Jacinta, Grace and Becky, I hope this thing called life keeps you all in my life forever.

To the lovers I have met and lost. You were lessons I did not think I needed to learn. Thank you for showing me that all the love I wanted to give you I should have given it to myself.

Lastly, I want to thank the Olympia Publishers team for believing in me and offering me this opportunity to share my writing with the world. Publishing my book has always been a dream of mine and you made that reality.

Introduction:
<u>Love, a subject difficult to grasp in just one poem</u>

I always had a feeling. A gloomy feeling surrounding my body, surrounding my mind. The feeling lingering, haunting me since I was only fifteen. Eighteen was the age when my soul was touched by her laugh. With that warm feeling of course came the shame and the tears. I was only a lost girl drowning in insecurities. At that age I knew what love was, but what loneliness felt like too. That feeling that love will be the death of me, I felt it so terribly deep. How many poets do you think had that feeling? The answer, do not give it to me now. Just think, think of Keats, think of Blake, but think of Dickinson too. My mother called Emily bland. Bland? Can you believe? That woman was bleeding love on paper. "Living in sin", hiding from the world must've been so tiring. Her poems, full of nothing but emotion. But who could read her? No one. Not even herself. Poets and their mystery — Nothing more beautiful. The questions after all these years we keep asking about them and how they were. The questions we will not stop asking. The answers they are not important. To feel everything so deeply can be such a blessing, oh but what a curse it can be. There are some people that call poets dramatic. Perhaps we are. Perhaps we just feel. We are all afraid of one angel. That angel is of course the angel of death. Perhaps us poets we are not afraid of life. To jump in the arms of love, nothing but bravery, or utter foolishness some would say. Being in love you are useless, nothing but a tool, a wondering fool.

As each numbered day passes, I see love for what it truly is. That love it did not belong to your face, I was wrong. You were the softest thing my eyes have laid on. I really did think you locked my heart and took the key. For so many years I felt nothing but trapped. All the souls my mouth has kissed had to be compared with you. My first poem about love belonged to you, I thought over you I would never get but here I am with a smile on my face writing my first poetry book and my heart has forgotten you completely.

For my mother's sleepless nights and wasted tears. I no longer bleed nor cry. I am finally smiling and so are you,

I love you the most, Mama.

1st Section:
Childhood love lectures

Childhood Love Lectures

I was five when I saw my mother cry for the first time.
helpless I would feel
my arms would surround her and the suffering found in
her voice would get greater as her cries would get louder.
since that gloomy day I never stopped wondering
wondering why she was fighting so hard for his attention
wondering why without him she felt so lost
wondering why she felt this pain was worth the cost.
ten years pass by and courage is found in me
I ask her why
why she stays
why she has accepted this torture for so long
why she doesn't want more
why he is still the only man she can adore
the answer has never been simpler for her
"I love him"
her response caused more confusion than clarity for me
the rage in my heart, with her I couldn't agree
the love I have seen in films
the love I read about in books
the love I was convinced I would die for, no doubt
that is not the love my mother was talking about.

Father, we had a good day

You took me fishing when I was six
The only moment I felt loved by you
You are preoccupied by the lovely view
The little fish in my hand, agitated
Will it live or die? I decide
I let it go, as soon as it touched my soft skin
For a change alcohol it is not your choice, you care about me
My soul felt calmness it had never felt before
It starts to rain, the waves get bigger
I felt nothing but safe
The yellow raincoat and your arms make everything feel okay
My innocent self for once nothing to worry about, no price to pay
We got home, the euphoria nowhere to be seen
The tension these walls have felt so many times
My mother's cries they have heard
Those memories, in the back of my brain, blurred
My soul knew, it knew that a good day will not change anything
Instead of feeling joy, smiling
I lay down on my bedroom floor,
Floods start running down my cheek
Only one question going through my mind
His little toy I always am, forced to play
Why can't everyday be like today?

Don't you get sad?

my mother, my light
I stare a bit longer into her drained eyes
that is where I see
her roots, the crystalline blue sea
I see the sleepless nights and the pain
the hopes and dreams that died
I see how hard from the world she tries to hide
despite all of this
for her life is nothing but a gift, pure bliss
I see the lovable smile and the wrinkles on her kind face
that she is still here I am nothing but glad
when you look at your parents for too long
don't you get sad?

See you soon, I hope

It took me some time
To write this poem for you
I don't really have a reason why
You are lonely, my heart hurts,
it makes me cry.

I could not find the right words
I was only a lost child
Next to me, you were always there
you raised me the best you could
you showed me that you care.

You gave me guidance
You gave me wisdom
I haven't seen your face in years
Every time I hear your voice over the phone
it is so hard to stop my tears.

I am terrified your old soul one day will not wake up
And I won't be there to say goodbye
And I won't be there to look into your gracious eyes
I hope this is nothing but a climb
I hope there is still time.

Two thousand miles between us

But I feel you close to me sometimes
The people were mean at first Grandma
They still are from time to time
about us they didn't give a dime.

As days go by
Time heals my wound
Grandma so much love in my heart for you
I hope I get to see you soon.

Beach side

I miss you
I miss your soft burning sand
Tears running down my cheek as I think
For six years I haven't stepped foot on that land.

I miss the limpid calming sea
I miss when things were simple
my friends and their kind faces
I miss the sound of my innocent giggle.

I miss when just one swim was the answer
Only happiness found in those days
All I needed
Was a gentle touch from your waves.

listening to the soothing waves of the sea
she kissed me
only ten years old, lost kids
in my mind, I was nothing but confused
I wondered what magic spell she used
she kissed me
a couple of harmless, young hearts
laying on the soft sand
she took me there, to Loveland

our head tilted watching the stars
she kissed me
I still remember the scar on your left knee
everything changed
although the moment,
full of joy
the shame and tears followed
so much pain I have swallowed
the loss of friendship came too
after that kiss, not a word shared with you
I wonder where you are
your voice I haven't heard in years
everything is different now
I no longer wish to be someone else
I am no longer scared
I wish more memories we shared
that kiss, the beginning of so many wars
from time to time, *I still think of those eyes of yours.*

how can this be
at the bottom of the sea
you are finally at peace
blue skies, rainbows
and blooming trees
the universe is too big, too great
your only option was to disappear
god can be seen from there
come back to them, your daughters

you belong here, not in the calming waters.

welcome back friend
suffering you have felt, for that to happen I did not intend
I have truly missed you
have you missed my touch?
I missed yours too much
spending your divine time running away from me
only for me to become the only thing you chase
in the end you realised, this was never a race
spending all your life looking for me
looking in so many places, after so many tries
only to find out I was nowhere but in front of your eyes.

-       *Coming back to Love.*

Moments and pictures

another moment passes by me
another moment I wish it lasted longer
I take a picture thinking that would help
as always, the feeling of regret is stronger.

pretty sky, to your beauty no one can compare
love for the angel of death I have too
the sea, the sky I wish I could kiss
oh, how I depend on you.

perhaps my phone can capture the smiles
the emotion, that is what I wish to keep forever
the warmth in my heart
take me to the land of love, take me wherever.

2nd Section:
Ghosts of past lovers

Each night the ending I felt it near
They tore my heart apart but the smile on my face, it is still here.

another perfect day, you and I

see me out your window,
for us nothing but blue **skies**
a younger soul but somehow more **wise**
the sun rays kiss your soft skin
switch eyes with me
see yourself with my **eyes**
hold my hand, the incertitude, it **dies**
you can have your way,
getting to know you, my favourite **book**
when I need advice, at your face I **look**
wash my sins my love
everything that comes out your mouth makes sense
you are music
your voice, a song I never get tired **of**
in the end I guess I found what it is, **love**.

Do you still dream about her?
— yes of course I do. I think I will always want her.
I constantly ask myself why her?
I think every fool that fell in love with someone who does
not love them back asks that question I suppose.
Her presence in my writing makes me feel less alone.
If it wasn't her would it be someone else? Or would I not

dream at all?
You see, if I do not dream her I feel as though sleeping was pointless.
Without her cherry flavoured kisses, life is nothing but joyless.
Pathetic I feel for wasting so much time thinking about her, I admit.
So, what's my other choice? Nothingness? The abyss?
I would rather have an illusion,
I got to call you mine for just one season
I love sleeping now and for only one reason
That for those peaceful hours I get,
my mind is occupied only by your kind face
I should stop haunting you and let you be
My darling one more time tell me that you love me.

Even if it is a lie
I want those little words to come out your mouth
I want to hear you say it one more time

Even if it is a lie
Let me in and give me but one clue
I want nothing but to be next to you

Even if it is a lie
I want your hand to hold
Do not leave me in the freezing cold

I am not what you want
I am nothing but shy
Let's give this another try
Even if it is a lie.

Two a.m. again staring at my glaring screen
Two a.m. again wondering what could've been
two months, no words from you
one day fate tortures me to see you again
speechless, paralyzed, I miss my train
you **smile.**
I don't.
you get **closer**
reminded you are a fraud, solely a poser
your arms around me, I feel nothing but **suffocated**
"*Are you trying to forget about me?*" you ask
our relationship toxic, nothing but a disaster

"*everyday*," so quickly I answer.

Holding her hand

You were never a good a lover
Nights. Lonely nights
Today we did good. No fights
You are sleeping next to me
While I?
I dream of her
Here in my dreams I am going in the calming sea, for a swim
I need a way out
No one left call
Never letting anyone in, never coming down, this wall
You asked me what I'm thinking about
"You," I answered
You smile
You say nothing for a while
Your honey eyes start shining
Naïve soul
Barefoot in the park,
Without her here I am afraid of the dark
I hold your hand, but after all this time
Hers is the one I am still reaching for
Turn me around one last time
Getting mad won't change a thing
If I asked you, would you agree?
The frustration, it is killing me.

for this moment I waited for so long
the band, they are playing our song
I pictured what it would feel like
I pictured magic
I pictured love felt so profound
magic was nowhere to be found
that night brought me only emptiness
my body soaked in fear
used I felt, I shared a tear
while you stood watching, opening another beer
the sun was rising, I heard the door shut
you left
I went straight in the shower
vulnerable, I was nothing but a fragile flower
the freezing cold water
washing my guilt away
a night hard to forget
a night leaving me alone drowning in regret.

you used to drive your mother's car just to see me
no driving license, that did not matter
love is selfish
I am nothing but greedy, I do not want to share
I want to see you all night, but about me you do not care
your new girl, she is cooler than me that I know
baby show me again how you feel down low.

To forgive you, I can't yet

You are in a different city
In my wondering heart you can be found
Thinking about you does not scare me any more
I no longer need to drown in wine
Dreaming here on my own that I did not expect
The knife
In my heart you placed it, so direct.

Perhaps one day I get to see your face again
Perhaps then I will not remember any pain
Without your hand holding mine, I am okay
I can breathe
Lessons you taught me
Lessons I did not want to discover
You never wanted for me to recover.

Forgiveness, we will leave it for another day
And although towards me
You were nothing but hateful
Changed for the better
With a smile on my face, I remain grateful.

your face I haven't seen in months
but my heart is still full of love for you

the bus drives past your avenue
the whole universe found in your smile
I miss it
with your whole body you give her love
thinking about you, that I am tired of
I am aware too many of my poems belong to you
my soul so much has bled
these lines in vain, to you I am nothing but dead.

You had to go

We shared one last kiss
Looking out the window
The pink sky I was admiring
Ignoring you, has become tiring.

Your violent stare follows me around the room
The end, it is near
Falling out of love, my greatest fear.

Out of my life you will leave
Things will be better without here
My bed, I will call my own again
Strangers, memories shared, all in vain.

In cold sweats I won't have to drown any more
We were close but not quite
Your honey-coloured eyes no longer my favourite sight.

you are here again

our love, missing excitement, plain
my love here we are, the same string, together again

my heart, put it back on the shelf
that night as always repeats itself

yours, you said I'd always be
this time, nothing is the same
no match can save this, it is gone, the flame,

your hand on my thigh I can feel the other girls it has touched
your soft lips, they make my heart sink
picturing all the souls they have kissed
on the left side of the bed, it missed you
no escape from your spell… what did I get myself into?

Where did you go?

No one makes me feel like you
Every day I try to find you in someone new
My first love, unrequited, a tragedy.

Know that if you did not touch me,
Kiss me the way you did, I
I would not feel this way
If you left my life, I would probably be okay.

I still picture you next to me staring into my hazel eyes
My love for you, I hope soon it dies
Some part of me, full of regret, wanted you to be mine
Loneliness I feel, all killed with the bottle of red wine.

Your presence, I do not want it to leave my life
Even though you can never love me
Even though your love belongs to someone else
I was mean, all I am asking is for you not to hate me
If I could erase who you thought I was
Our love story would end in applause.

They said love does not come easy
Biking to her house I picked her a daisy
I should not feel this much, this early

My eyes laying on the softest thing
For her this is nothing but a fling
Silly expectations broke my heart once again
I only have eyes for her
Sweet like honey she was
I was too blind to see
That in the end she'll sting like a bee.

We want to know what **love** is
We do not desire to look into it too deep
the ignorance we adore and would like to stay asleep
We want to know what **love** is
terrified we are
terrified that true love is nothing but rare
so rare that if too long we look for it nothing will be there
lovelessness, the only alternative
fear in our heart, hesitation
causing nothing but frustration
with doubt in our mind, the chance at it we might miss
We want to know what **love** is.

About us I still don't know how you feel
Each night I wonder if any of this is real
Perhaps the truth I do not want to find out
Perhaps the silence I prefer
My heart shatters knowing I will never be her
I like to think I am your favourite girl
Your favourite pair of eyes that you lie to
Show me what I need to do
To be adored by you.

reach for my hand again
do not let our love go down the drain
follow me into the infinity darling
can you not see you were the only one I ever desired?
are you not tired?
tired of running away from love?
tired of running away from us?
stop being hesitant, do not make a fuss
with me by your side, you would be stronger
we are young romantic fools
terrified no longer.

Too serious

I would do everything different
If I had the chance to talk to you again
Lies I have told you, nothing to gain
I'd tell you the truth from day one
I wish I was more wise
Wisdom for you I wish I had
Writing these words, they make me but one thing, sad
Do not take life too seriously like you always do
Time is yours, no one is after you
Young and lost we were
It is over now
That makes me nothing but glad
Your tears won't mean anything in a year that I promise
You will see
Life you will be able to live it, without me
I hope you forget my name
The pain I have caused I hope you forget that too
Some part of me is full of regret
Some part of me wishes you were the one I adore
But this is not the love I longed for.

today
I remember you were always so smart
flowers **bloom** from my heart

sharing one last kiss, maybe
two years gone since the day you broke me
happy **sorrow anniversary** baby
touch me one last time, show me how

- *Do you still love me? say it now.*

- *Flowers will bloom from this chaos.*

a kiss on my cheek, I still hear your violent "adieu"
I never thought I'd be here without you
it felt permanent
my wondering mind thinking of our first kiss, on the dancefloor
your gentle, vulgar face does not scare me any more
I smile
towards me you sent it only hate
and despite of it all I am glad this was my fate
a scar on my heart you left
a new me I had to rebuild
before sleep I don't need to wear your sweater
without you here, I am myself, I am better.

taxi journey

just another late night out
this time I might not carry the doubt
the street lights, for you baby, they are shining
can they shine forever? I want to stop growing

looking out the window
my attention still on the lights, they pass by me
I notice everything, so does she
in my heart nothing but joy
a moment, I hope it will never end
then you cross my mind, my weekend friend.

you kiss my hand
falling for you was not at all planned
maybe a chance at happiness I should take
we are close of getting in, passed the queue
nothing but love is served at table forty-two.

my face, no longer enough for you
not what you want. you keep telling me
we get along, stop your crying
you get close and whisper in my ear
"my love it will only get worse from here".

12:36 a.m., I want to go home, I would rather be alone
cold, soaked in sweat, I would rather be on my own
I wish I could fix you
I wish you could see me
I wish in my arms you would feel nothing but free.

that night, your best friend gave you a tattoo
you let him stick and poke your skin
in your bedroom
I thought in the end you were going to let me in
in the morning, we went back to your silly games
happiness only found in the picture frames.

I do not need to pray, I just need to look at your face
my darling, you are the only thing I chase
barefoot on the beach, you are running away
selfish, reckless, I have become, you make me this way.

in my eyes you won't look, I want to get lost in yours
flowers, I have sent to your door
for once, turn my body around
silence, all you give me, blue the only emotion, ready to drown.

Take me there

our first date, the night garden
to you I felt nothing but a burden
mesmerised, flowers of all colours surround us
a yellow rose you're offering me
I did not notice the thorns your soft skin was carrying
I cannot take my eyes off the view,
a butterfly on your nose and your gleaming smile
your irresistible style
this place you called lonesome
I never knew why
always the smart one, empty and tough
happy we are, for you it is not enough
no one can give me what you gave me
like you ,there is no one
but like me, you can find many
insignificant we were
out of the blue on us you decided to quit

your last words, "not worth it".

I could tell you that I like you
I don't think that's what you want to hear
young and lost, we should run away and disappear
obsessed I am not, I promise

as soon as I show emotions, scared you will get
let's put this to an end. it is not too late yet
my therapist would not be proud of me if I dwell on this
it will be on my mind for a while, your kiss
one date was enough and we know it
the situation I admit, not ideal
perhaps the second one would make this feel *too real.*

- *first and last date.*

I no longer wish to **mourn** over a love that was never there
asking, begging, for someone who does not care
the freckles between your eyes, the **scar** on your right knee
a **prisoner** under your spell I no longer wish to be
your love, I want it
you were nothing but a bad liar
to be loved by me, that is **my biggest desire.**

Saviour to no one

Everything was different with you
You would push me away
My reflection I am ashamed of, why am I begging you to stay?
I want you more
I am hurt, you tell me repeatedly
No sign of fear in my bones
Meet me at our spot, next to the gas station
I can be your salvation
Let me in for once
Affectionate
Warm you call me
But is it all enough for you?
Those mean words you uttered, are they true?
A place in your heart I do not want
A distant thought I would like to become
I am so easy to forget
Immune to pain, my heart no longer upset.

Let me show you love
Love you have never seen before
Promise I will not be a bore.

Let me be yours

Absence of sins
You open your mouth and heaven sings.

Let me hold you in my arms
Like you have never been hold
Your heart let me treat it like gold.

To be your Mary Magdalene
Your pure angel
My love, do not become another stranger.

Page turned on me and you.

A liar. I was one
From the moment things got real for you, I was done
"I love you," you said
I did not say it back
Just like everything else, this ending for you was an attack.

Always taking things so personal
I hated that about you
Your fear, losing me, came true.

I got to know you too well
You loved me more, I could tell
I want to still want your presence around me
Everything is consumed.

Those three little words should've never come out my cursed mouth
They have no meaning now
To keep loving you, I don't know how
I let you down
I am okay with that.

access to me I will no longer offer you
I won't let you rub salt on my old wounds

no more fights or wasted afternoons
you put me through nothing but hell
and still I stayed by **your side**
loved you just for you to hate me
ending up on different paths
time to do something better with **my life.**

nothing changes, every day is the same
nervous I still get at the mention of your name
naive I was, thinking it meant so much more
bad things are temporary, it is true
but all good things come to an end too.

these days all I feel is rage
claustrophobic
impatient
looking for a way out, out of this cage.

to draw you I tried
to draw you as **the villain** I wanted, but couldn't
I drew you as a peaceful day
in my dreams, my love, I'm still *asking you to stay.*

never yours

too much too handle
lost, rushing, chasing forced feelings
look into my eyes tell me what's in there
disordered hearts you and I, what a pair.

you want to get to know me
tell me under my skin what you found
last time you tried to love me, half of you drowned.

you were trying to get better and I left you
full of guilt I felt
we'll cross paths again and my heart in your hands will melt.
nothing wrong with wanting more I know that now
without you, life gave me many opened doors
honey, in the end I was *never yours*.

no song would make sense without you
end the mind games my love, give me one clue
my heart drowning in nothing but passion
passion for those magical eyes and contagious smile
rushing, not an option, we need to give fate a while
I try to write about love and words can't help to fail me
I wish my dreams you could see

you would see nothing but our hands holding
since I met you, a new me you started moulding.

- *Who was I before meeting you?*

- *We will bloom soon.*

My body, remodelled since meeting you

I met you in the dark, smoke in your tired eyes
This mayhem, look my dear it got us so far
This, only the start, too good to be true sometimes
For your divine stare, I could commit so many crimes

Body modification, your mark I want it on me
A part of you on my skin, eternal
Smile, feels good to be wanted by you
You loved me for so long, your fantasies they all came true.

Soon, my heart will be yours to take
Please do not break it
I know you are scared, so am I
Nothing going for us, let's give this a try.

Looking up and see your face
My head on your chest
I hear your breathing and know I am not alone
Do not half love me
Love me with everything
or don't give me anything.

- *My favourite everything, my sunflower.*

Time, it should end

Twenty years old, an adult I am supposed to be
A child I would like to be again, stare at it, the limpid sea
Feeling nothing but lost
You're in my bed, I wish someone else would call my phone
A message to her, innocent gesture, I will send
Things quickly I need to end
All I did used to be for you
I wanted to be your everything
Now, our love story can be anything
This car journey feels like it will never end
With you, feeling trapped, controlled
Open the door, I can throw myself into the freezing cold
The snow would surround my body, the thinking will stop
I saw the future with you
Time? Can I stop it?
Thirty years later and the answer was no
No sign of change still surrounded by the violent snow
We are sitting in front of the fire on different sofas
Old, wrinkled souls who were never able to love
Our soulmates perhaps have been misplaced

What a waste.

my dear friend,
there is no need to look for love
I promise,
love is always with you
love is gentle, love remains like a tattoo
love in each cup of coffee
love in each story
love in the morning or late at night
love in each poem you write
love is there to repair
look for it, love is everywhere.

a letter to my door you sent
started with a violent
"I miss you"
you called me special,
for my innocent mind that was enough
I am but a romantic fool
you were nothing but cruel
sitting here impatiently, drowning in doubt
you said you love me but that was the last time you reached out.

one night, it felt so real
me in the passenger seat, you at the steering wheel
your silhouette in the morning sun
your gentle touch
I have seen an angel
perhaps she is more, a goddess
you showed me nothing but tenderness
still searching for those sparks of happiness.

I treat you with **silence**
it is killing me, this deafening violence
we are wasting time ignoring each other
pretending
in front of our eyes, in shambles, we can see it ending
sharing conversations with you,
that is how this time should be spent
I called you a coward, wrong I was, it is not what I meant
I saw your kind grin, you asked, **"Is it better to speak or die?"**
your voice, I wish I could hear it one last time
to tell you I have the answer **now**
brave enough in the end, I wish for a riot
I no longer choose the **quiet**
by not saying how you feel, your life is nothing but ruined
I want to feel it again, the heat of your breath

all left for me now, a lonely *death*.

I picture you
Your charismatic smirk
Your red velvet dress
Finally, my love for you I confess.

Your elegant voice,
It touches my soul
Serenading French songs
Our story nothing but a mess, full of rights and wrongs.

In the reflection of the window
I see the sunset
In my projections, the only place you are seen
Another day wasted thinking about what could have been.

Illusion

My first life, wasted, trapped in your heart
Dreams, with you I had none
Finally, awake, a new me now
I need to move on, just not sure how
Special, you really are
You do not see what I see, which is frustrating
It takes time that's what they say
Your truest self, you will see it one day
I adore you, I really do
In your reach, I am no longer
For now, to be strangers again we must choose
I will be rooting for you no doubt
Rooting for those glowing eyes and warm smile
Apart we need to be, to grow, all this hurt will be worthwhile.

Ignored by lover

emotionless, I feel
a loner before you, maybe I needed to heal
something has happened
I ask, no words come from your mouth
my poor brain wondering
wondering, I cannot close my eyes
maybe I want this to be the end, the flame dies.

my body you knew it like it was yours
for your attention I have to fight
no hope for us, nowhere to be seen, the light
give me time
each moment surrounded by your kind smile I will cherish
your face from my mind will fade, and with it our love will perish.

my energy all trapped inside of you
while you waste yours on someone else
every day you promised a happy ending we will get
one more lie, and our eyes for the last time have met.

How you felt that day

Am I on your mind?
Do you still hate me for leaving you behind?

Did you hope I cried myself to sleep?
Did you hope I felt the wound just as deep?

Do you think about the person I am without you?
Did you hope I found someone new?

Amusing I find it, that I think about your face
We were missing the spark, the wow
I wonder what you would say if you could see me now.

control, it does not belong to me
a fickle soul I came across
our chaotic story nothing but a loss
around you, I cannot trust myself
each gift you buy me means nothing
each argument makes me fall in love with you
in the end, our biggest worry became true
no other option but to leave you behind
my head tilted, starry sky, I am nothing but an empty mind.

\-   *Empty Mind.*

afraid of change
after all these years, my darling doesn't it feel strange?
paralysed, in the same place for so long
you keep pushing me away
talking about needing space
you remind me I am so easy to replace
around you I never feel good enough
a war in your mind, you're telling me I need to hold on
in your arms, that is where I belong.

A fragment of a moment
All it took
For you to become my muse
My heart,
I let you abuse.

Lately I feel like I am in the way
I am no longer what you desire
Perhaps my fear, it is in my head
All I want, you and I
forever in this bed.

You avoid looking into my eyes
Our pages you decided to burn
Your picture I refuse to erase

It is not too late
one last time meet me at **our place.**

another morning waking up wondering
if only your soul, I could hold it in my hands
realising it all belongs to me, the blame
it was not just my doomed fate
the walls I can never bring down
the walls I bring down for the wrong person
always in the wrong season
for once the one apologising is me
I'm sorry
things could've been so great
just like a movie you could have been the best part
but it all crumbled in front of us and with it **my heart.**

- *Lights, cameras and heartbreak.*

After Saturday Night

Happiness.
The only emotion I should be feeling
I cry
All the wars inside my head ignored, I kiss your thigh.

For you, everything between us is perfect
Silly girl
You watch me swimming in your pool
You bore me, I thought you were cool.

In my daydreams you were better
Reality offering me constant disappointment
Your style, your vocabulary,
Nothing about you excites me, scary.

Your jealousy I can sense
Making love to you but she
She is my muse
The muse I need to entertain, the one I need to amuse.

I go to her sometimes
The girl in my projections
Out of this world, no comparison, divine
She lays down next to me, the stars align.

thinking about you only when I was lonely
your muse you called me, pure and holy
I cared about you,
not the way you wanted me to
I cared, but only in minor doses
in, I finally let you after your failed tries
and games of persuasion
me? I am no longer,
you?
the only thing I see when I look in my reflection
do not make me feel bad just because I want your affection
yours to obtain, mission complete
my tears keeping me company on this empty *street*.

A dream of you
A year has passed,
The mixed signals, I miss them, the chase
Yours is still the face
The face I adore
Those blue eyes of yours appear in my dreams sometimes
A far away memory you are
For some reason you occupy my mind, all in vain
Your attention I would love to get it again
Our story, brief, but your absence I feel it deeply
I miss talking to you
Hearing your suave voice
Seeing your charming smile
Your stare that makes anyone weak

Everything about you, mystique
What could have been? The question I always ask
Sweet heaven, one of the possible answers
We could have been depressive
A disaster, a violent spark, aggressive
After all this time I am but one thing, confused
Confused as to why my lines of poetry still belong to you
You belong to her that I know,
I am but a fool, wish my brain would fixate on someone new.

About us I still don't know how you feel
Each night I wonder if any of this is real
Perhaps the truth I do not want to find out
Perhaps the silence I prefer
My heart shatters knowing I will never be her
I like to think I am your favourite girl
Your favourite pair of eyes that you lie to
Show me what I need to do
To be adored by you.

Another late night spent in your bed

My heart so many times you left it bruised
Your hand holding mine, I feel nothing but used

Tenderness I wish you would show me

Red candles on your nightstand
The cherry scent gives me hope
Hope that you will no longer be distant
Hope that for once you will listen.

You were trying to get better
I wonder if you're still wearing my sweater

That is when I left your life
You said to keep in touch
I refused
Out of the blue, you were nothing but confused

There were moments
when I thought I wanted you back
With my mind I had to fight
In the end maybe you were right

If souls to intertwine with you do not find
Would history repeat itself?
Would we go back to the start?
Or would we once again fall apart?

After all this time
I am still failing
The only one I am still chasing
Incapable of figuring you out
Where it all went wrong I still cannot work out
You still hit me up on strange occasions
Memories we shared, I still avoid those locations
I wonder if your friends know about me
I wonder without my presence do you finally feel free?

3rd Section:
My younger self is smiling

*fo*rgive yourself
for letting them treat you the way they did
the **anger** will not help anyone
it will cause more damage
you will find a way to manage
it will **hurt**
hurt
And **hurt** some more
one day the tears will stop I promise
the pain a distant memory will become
you will finally bloom my cherished plum.

My past self is smiling
She feels nothing but relieved
She sees that I have healed
She sees that I am still healing
She sees that I have not stopped dreaming
She sees I no longer need to be sedated
She sees I can eat without sharing tears and feeling guilty
She sees that I feel pretty
She sees me smiling too
She sees the ground so many times I hit
She sees that I did not quit
***She** sees me saying that I love life and mean it.*

Waking up

You woke up
Do not look at your glaring screen just yet
This advice I too sometimes forget

Pause for one second
Lift your head off your pillow
Smile while you look out your window

Sip your coffee and just stare at the sun
Forget about the day that is so far
Think about who you truly are

Think of the progress you made
Think of how you no longer want to be numb
Think of how great you have become

Think of how many times to live you were scared
Think of how many tears you shared
But think of how all of this was worth it.

dream, do not let it end
you deserve more
this life, great things has planned for you
destined to be someone great, that is something you

always knew.

those tiny demons, they tell you to stop
don't you dare ever give in
ignorant no longer, just aware
the answer has always been
a dream and some air.

staring at your posters on the wall
your name? one day it might appear on one
and if not? what then?
do not panic, do not start screaming
hope, do not let it die until you can no
longer be dreaming.

the universe might be too bright
everything can be gone in one second
life is nothing but fragile
an everlasting battle
despite all of this
with each soft kiss from the sun
you still keep going you are still trying.

Healing

each morning started with a peaceful moment
wandering mind, my natural endowment
rainbow in the sky,
surrounded by its power
one with the earth just like a flower
your name I thought my brain had forgotten
I was terribly wrong
the journey of healing, difficult one
the journey, it is not a straight line
hard to accept I still have tears to share for you
the pain will slowly be gone from my heart
me glowing, that will be my favourite *piece of art*.

I am starting to finally learn
It is more than okay to outgrow people
Not a tragedy or a sense of evil
No hate shared for them
Any obstacle, we will overcome
Being apart, the best decision
For now, they slow down your vision
Take deep breaths
Life for you both has so many winnings
It is time for new beginnings.

keep watering your plants
keep being a dreamer
writer, do not forget to be a reader
keep showing people that you care
keep living unaware
nothing to gain, nothing to lose
relax, no rush to decide
just enjoy the ride.

self-love, a thing you can no longer condemn
drop **them**
those little things you're holding onto
the **seeds**
follow where this unknown leads
water **them**
avoid the obstacle, the pothole
cleanse your **soul**
from this madness something will grow, that is true
and that will be *you*.

Growth

Growth, it does not come easy
Growth, it will bring you floods of tears
Growth will make you wonder if it's worth it
Growth will make you face your fears.

Growth, it will bring you discomfort
Growth, it will bring you down to your knees
Growth will bring you sleepless nights
Growth will make you feel at ease.

Do not let them bring you down
Keep moving at your own pace
Be curious, but do not hurry
Deep breaths, look around this is not a race.

Fear
My brown tired eyes open
The only emotion my tummy knows
Fear.
I do not want to grow
What the future holds, I do not want to know
I drink and smoke maybe that will help
Maybe that will stop the time
But it doesn't
Can no longer call myself a student

Half of my identity is gone
Maybe I will end up a tragedy just like the Black Swan
I do not have dreams
Maybe that is the issue
Maybe that is why I feel so lost
I can work hard for something, is it worth the cost?
Can I be a writer without writing?
Can I be a poet without composing poems?
Can I be a screenwriter without working on screenplays?
I do not wish to do anything
I wish to do everything
No direction here
Life always a mystery, nothing is clear
I know that is the last thing you want to hear
But all is not lost
Hold on to hope
Love is everywhere if you look for it
And where there's love there is everything
See the light, do not miss your chance, pick up the phone when it will ring.

I want to believe in you
With my entire being I really do
It is hard
Hard to believe you truly are love
When all these years
All you brought me was nothing but shame and fear
There were moments I felt you near

But after all these years your existence remains unclear
Feeling lost that I am sick of
My empty heart I think it needs your presence
I do not know how to let you in
Perhaps I will never find out
Perhaps until my last breath my mind will remain in doubt.
I wonder as angels caress my skin

- *God will I ever let you in?*

Friends I have lost

Friends I have lost
I think of the ones that broke my heart
Tonight, my mind occupied by memories
Would things be different if all this time we were not apart?

How the days would've been, it is all a mystery
I think of the ones that I hurt too
Some, on days like this I do miss
Without them, I shine that is true.

I am still rooting for them
I send them light their way
Loneliness does not scare me any more
I do hope we meet again someday.

blood, it is not everything
biology does not limit us
some abandoned, it gets ugly
we are not all lucky
we have to forget about our ego and our pride
we have the freedom to decide
a choice for a community
full of nothing of love and joy

where there is no need for performing nor pretending

being yourself, it is more than enough

no longer the need to despair in loneliness and agony
you can choose your family.

Coffee for dinner

four a.m. on a Monday morning
my eyes are begging to be closed
my stomach begging to be fed
instead, I get out of bed
tears in my eyes I start running
feeling the sweat dripping on my skin
knowing calories, I will burn
will I ever escape? will I ever learn?
the joy I feel cannot compare
drowned in compliments about my figure
my fifth cigarette of the day
my time wasted again in a café
the euphoria, it is gone
food, my mouth hasn't tasted in days
I am nothing but a loser
the empty feeling making me feel like a winner
nothing changes, coffee for dinner.

If tomorrow does not come

If tomorrow does not come
I will dance the old blues in the rain
If tomorrow does not come
I did not live in vain.

If tomorrow does not come
One more time I will get dressed
If tomorrow does not come
I know I tried my best.

If tomorrow does not come
I will think about my girlhood
If tomorrow does not come
I loved as hard as I could.

With peace in my heart
A cup of coffee in my hand
My mouth full of bubble-gum
I will smile
If tomorrow does not come.

embrace your darkness
make her your friend
no need to think ahead
deep breaths, new beginnings
there is magic inside of you
I hope you will find it soon
let yourself glow like the moon.

nights like these I still wonder
two sugars in my warm tea
I wonder if I'm still the old me
I wonder if I made any progress at all
I wonder if the path to my old ways I should take
perhaps I miss pretending, being fake
healing, it is not linear, that I know
but nights like these I wonder if I should just let go
the moon listens, and she reminds me tonight
the power I have as a mortal made of light.

It's **okay**.
Take everything day by day
Things, they do seem **hopeless** right now
I know
But the world will smile again
The **sun** will be seen after this storm, after this rain
In your mind there will be no war

And in the end, we will start **dancing** once more.

I feel safe in my room again
My lungs no longer scared to breathe
The monsters under my bed they no longer stare
The skeletons in my closet they help me pick what to wear
My own company I enjoy thoroughly
I dreamt
and dreamt of this day for so long

and it is finally here.

growing older
the clarity of my dreams, foggier
my violent thoughts, louder
I want to do everything,
read every book,
listen to every song
they keep on telling me to hold on and be strong
I want to be everywhere
so much I have not yet conquered
running out of time, my days are numbered
fragile, on the verge of breaking
nothing holding me together but this lean suture
falling into the arms of the uncertain future.

sweet November
you brought me tears in the dark
you brought me late **nights**
sometimes in the morning too
war in my mind, violent **fights**.

sweet November
surrounded by my family's smiles
their love I felt it **deeply**
you brought me warm nights
getting lost in your nostalgic vibrancy **completely.**

goodbye sweet November
perhaps you will be **missed**
perhaps not
grateful that by you I have been **kissed.**

December, joy in my heart I hope you will bring
Be gentle with my **precious mind**
Please **be kind.**
(14 November 2020, 22:47 p.m.)

In self-hatred I used to drown

No hand to hold on my way down
Now that only love in my heart can be found
Now that I am not anyone's toy
They try and take my joy
They like to call me selfish
Selfish as creating boundaries does not seem fair
Selfish as for once about me I care.

My teenager years I spent them being afraid
Trapped
Reality for so long I tried to evade.

No longer a slave to my own thoughts
No longer a prisoner to the waves of the sea
Now I finally feel free.

That I am still here I cannot believe
Out of my head
My brain for so long wanted me dead.

I wish life would move slow
Each moment so quickly passes
I wonder if there is enough time to grow.

You are never on your own

Even in the moments
When there is no one left to call
The day is waiting patiently for you
The sun dying of excitement to caress your delicate skin
Pay no mind to what has been
The birds thrilled to serenade your cherished soul
It is okay, some things are not in our control
While flowers bloom out of your chest
Sometimes difficult to see
How much you have grown
I promise you are not on your own.

Deep breaths, it is time for new beginnings
Things, do not take them personal
Through the state of chaos
The sunrise made you feel blessed
Be joyous, for trying your best
Be proud, for enduring so much pain
Be grateful, for the chance to start again.

The days darkness is nowhere to be seen

The days, where light is the only thing found in my heart
The days, when it's time for her to depart
I try my hardest not to scream
I try my hardest to accept this is not just a dream
For so long darkness was the only thing keeping me company
Now she rarely comes to visit
This, sometimes could be nothing but terrifying
Hard to believe in end I have stopped my crying.